stowaway

Peter J M Clive

Words by Peter J M Clive

Glasgow, Scotland

All Rights Reserved

Copyright © Peter J M Clive 2022

ISBN: 978-1-4717-3922-4

Imprint: Lulu

stowaway

Forces of aggression, ideology and greed isolate us from each other:
Peter Clive's second poetry collection, "stowaway," explores the
human experience of shared pain and expresses solidarity with
refugees and the victims of war, imperialism and poverty.

Peter J M Clive

Peter lives on the southside of Glasgow, Scotland with his wife and their three children. He is a scientist who has worked in the renewable energy sector for nearly two decades. As well as poetry, he enjoys composing music for the piano and spending time in the Isle of Lewis and St Andrews with family.

His first poetry collection, "the end of the age of fire," about climate change. was published to coincide with COP26 and is currently available. "stowaway" is his second collection.

Acknowledgements

"August 9th, 1945," "Secondary target," and "Caesium 137" first appeared in the Dove Tales project "In the Shadow of the Bomb": https://www.dovetalesscotland.co.uk/intheshadowofthebomb

"Cuneiform" first appeared in Culture Matters: https://www.culturematters.org.uk/index.php/arts/poetry/item/2972 -ach-well-all-livin-language-is-sacred-an-appreciation-of-tom- leonard

"Grenfell" first appeared in Writers' Café Magazine issue 12 "Truth and Lies": https://thewriterscafemagazine.wordpress.com/2018/09/16/the- writerscafe-magazine-issue-12-truths-and-lies/

"Seven balloons at sunset" first appeared in the Festival 2018 collection "Beyond Boundaries"

"The experiment" first appeared in Issue 5 of The Rush: https://www.rushmagazine.org/february-2020

"The fire" first appeared in Seahorse Publications' anthology "Glasgow: Historical City"

"The magic money tree" first appeared in Writers' Café Magazine issue 11 "Into the Trees": https://thewriterscafemagazine.wordpress.com/2018/08/16/the- writers-cafe-magazine-issue-11-into-the-trees/

"The two masters" first appeared in Slant 34, Summer 2020

"Zapruder 313" first appeared in Dodging the Rain, March 2019: https://dodgingtherain.com/2019/03/

Contents

Literal interpretation

In Matthew 4:19 the Master said

"Follow me and I will make you fishers of men,"

and straightaway the disciples put down their nets

and left their homes. He did not mean

raising from the sea the dead bodies

of those who left their homes in Syria

only to find they could not walk on water.

The siege

"What is hateful to you, do not do to your neighbour. That is the whole Torah. The rest is commentary. Go and learn."

– Hillel the Elder

I don't remember when it began.

Alaric had just sacked Rome?

They had just buried Rankovic?

Or was it later, when Sloba spoke

about enemies within and without?

I don't recall. There was a storm

beneath a clear blue sky, and after it

all the colour had drained from the world

leaving a stark monochrome reality:

your existence threatened mine, mine yours.

Every nuance congealed and stiffened

into mutual exclusivity and zero sum.

Give and take could no longer coincide.

It had to be one or the other,

which in reality just meant take,

because who gives anything away

for nothing in return. My enemy's enemy

was with us or against us

as barbarians crossed the frontier

and friends became comrades

or were shot for cowardice or treason.

We built a city on a hill. We built a wall

around the city. We retreated behind the wall.

It was an ark, but being men, not gods,

we brought war, not water, into the world,

though we claimed to cleanse it all the same,

with muddy trenches, making mothers cry.

We were the flood for each other's vessel,

with no power to make the deluge desist,

only an urge to hold the other under

until the bubbles stopped. In our victory

we discovered all we had won was solitude

and regret, unsought, alone and lonely,

among the rigid and inflexible categories

of all the descriptions we had defended,

all the non-negotiable nonsense

for which we had fought and died,

the dilapidated scaffold we had raised

to build the hulls that enclosed our minds

and set them afloat upon a sea of discord.

They say do unto others, but I say do not.

Be guided by peace, not pleasure. Ask first

what would you not have done unto you,

and in accordance with that, leave things be.

In amnesiam[1]

The parade passes the monument:

they acknowledge the heroes,

lay down the memorial wreathes,

and after a decent interval

the crowds quietly disperse.

I linger for a while

among the cut flowers

and in death's dark bower

one steel grey November day

think on those they forget,

remember those never remembered,

think about their inglorious guilt,

their egregious acts and omissions,

cowardice, desertion, open atrocities

or moments of private hesitation precipitating worse

which they could have prevented, had they acted,

when fear or weakness or exhaustion

stole them from our high regard.

---

[1] Written on the occasion of Remembrance Day

Their ghosts wait for us in oblivion

where we will join them eventually

once our own victories wilt,

and borders for which we fought

are redrawn or abolished or forgotten,

and whatever cause we won that day

is finally lost to obscurity.

Our temporary triumphs

were good while they lasted,

but we must take our place

beside the monsters and the cannibals

in the shadows at last.

I think about the unknown and dismembered:

unremarkable, unremembered boys without posterity,

silently removed in pieces from the field,

without the utterance of a single word, then or now,

whose anonymous body parts my imagination reassembles

as cowards and traitors, to stumble and crawl

through my muddy mind in disorder.

Have I lived a good life?

Have I been a good man?

The answer rides a butterfly through this cemetery,

rises out of reach, flies along barbed wire borders

where ricochets sing, through wastelands

where every lost cause is still contested

and the mouth of no cannon can announce

on whose side of the border

it finally settles.

Kino I

Only sadism could relieve the tedium

of their unchallenged privilege,

and so they entertained themselves

with arbitrary evils. War, famine,

and pestilence served as distractions,

horsemen manoeuvred

with knight's move afterthought

across distant criss-crossed time zones

and continents that tiled the masquerade

in their villas and cavernous chateaux.

The planet was a Riviera casino

for their casual coin toss apocalypses:

billions of lives placed on red or black,

billions of minds taught right and wrong,

lies rolled like dice to cascade through their press.

A roulette wheel of diagnoses for their disorder

was attempted by the wise, to rattle in our intellect:

psychopathy, narcissism, dialectical materialism,

none ever quite discerning the root cause: nothing,

the green pocket that gives the house its edge,

the fathomless, oceanic, unending boredom,

that accompanied their vast, purposeless wealth,

fuel to their toxic and ineffably remote indolence.

They withdrew to their yachts

as history broke in waves upon the shore

where the Rights of Man were written on the sand,

under their indifferent and occasional glance

while they sipped their quarterdeck cocktails,

for they were impatient for the End of Days.

They had a concession agreement for the Rapture.

After all, the foyer is where the money is made.

Casabianca 2021[2]

The boy stood in the sinking boat
in which from war he fled.
The waves that o'er the gunwale broke
filled all therein with dread.

Yes, beautiful and bright he stood,
but could not rule the storm,
nor, crueller than the cold wind's blast,
the bitter bigots' scorn.

The waves rolled in - he could not go
without the coastguard's aid.
Some called them on the radio
as others hoped and prayed.

They called "Mayday Mayday Mayday,
we're tempest-tossed and drenched,"
and then they heard the coastguard say
"you ought to try the French".

---

[2] 27 refugees drowned in the English Channel when their dinghy sank on 24th November 2021, including at least three children.

"Please help us," once again they cried.

"so we may yet be gone!"

– And but the static hiss replied.

and fast the waves rolled on.

I could go on. and tell of how.

in lyrics fine and fair.

he look'd from that lone post of death.

in still yet brave despair.

but those who sing of splendour wild

we're never really there.

the faithful. gallant. noble child

described from their armchair

a myth. His needless sacrifice

did not empire preserve.

It is the cost of fear and lies

which nobody deserves.

Tank commander[3]

People always disappoint us

and yet we still love them.

We love them as individuals

and in the abstract, as ideals,

carrying slogans on placards,

building barricades, defending them,

shoulder to shoulder, singing

in praise of our infinite possibilities,

imagined futures of freedom and justice,

that we speak of in a single voice.

I sometimes wonder if the allure

of those infinite possibilities, for me,

is the possibility of escape they offer

from my limited reality of exclusion

and solitude, ostracism and loneliness.

Do I love them merely not to hate them?

Do I find in the great cause a surrogate

---

[3] Written on the 32nd anniversary of the 1989 Tiananmen Square protests and massacre

for practical fellowship withheld from me

among their everyday transactions,

wrapping myself in political pamphlets

because I feel like the discarded packaging

of pleasures they consume without thinking?

While they soar like eagles in imagined futures

I remain trapped in the cockpit of the present,

so when they stand in front of me,

asking me to join them, to step out of my tank,

abandon my post, and take up their struggle,

I know they aren't really talking to me.

They are talking to an imaginary person

that could join them in that imaginary future,

and I know that is not possible,

because that person doesn't exist. And then

I remember another comradeship and solidarity

that came from wearing a uniform

and when the order comes, I find it easy

to lift my foot off the clutch pedal

and let the tread roll over them.

People always disappoint us

and yet we still pretend to love them.

I can't pretend anymore. Someone else

will have to pretend for me from now on,

and I will do whatever they say I must

to help keep up that pretence.

The pity

There is more to condemn in this world

than there is time for censure,

more to celebrate than there is time for praise,

and in between we fall to rancour,

and the points we strenuously argue

only prove how little we have learned

about this world, and how little we know

about each other. We presume to speak for others

and yet remain strangers to ourselves,

are quick to raise our voice in indignation

but stay silent when what is required is remorse,

assemble to denounce criminals but grieve alone,

while forgetting we should all pity and be pitied

for there is more to condemn in this world

than there is time for censure,

more to celebrate than there is time for praise.

Tether

The fire and flood,

the plague in our blood,

the rich in the sky,

while poor drown and die

or struggle for breath:

those who dodge death

to orbit aspire[4]

while Earth is on fire,

and I truly hope

the virus and smoke

that makes millions choke

is found out in space.

When you win your race

the ribbon's a noose

for all the abuse,

and every excuse

twists into a rope.

---

[4] Bezos, Branson, Musk, *et al.*

Flourish[5]

"Welcome to Glasgow, delegates.

Here is our Glasgow coat of arms.

See, the bird, the tree, the bell, the fish?

And we have a story to tell about each,

but none that you might already know,

nothing about saints and kings from long ago.

We've updated them for contemporary relevance,

so: here is today's bird that never flew

because habitat change overtook it;

today's tree that never grew

but burned down in a wildfire instead;

today's bell that never rang,

because there was no point,

why would you ring an alarm

when we've ignored every other warning;

and the fish that never swam, but perished

in oceans swollen by melting ice, crimson with algae,

and turned acidic by our industries' exhaust fumes.

While you are here please give us a new tale to tell,

---

[5] An imagined address to the delegates attending COP26 in Glasgow

about how you solved what we don't need a saint to fix,

because none of us are saints, after all,

and it really doesn't take a miracle

to write a story about birds that fly and trees that grow

and fish that swim and bells that ring in celebration

of a future in which we let the whole world flourish."

Storm in a teacup

A lord, over a cup of tea,
of crisis and emergency
in his morning paper read
and "storm in a teacup" said,
to diminish its significance,
and justify indifference.

but while he stirred his tea and sipped,
the climate curdled, seasons slipped,
cyclones swirled, tipping points tipped,
and forests burned down to the ground
while frightened people looked around
for second chances, but time was up,

and somewhere, from a larger cup
a dark lord of inestimably higher rank
deep draughts of dire disaster drank.

Headhunters

We have shrunk so small
we live our lives in snow globes
and travel on ships in bottles
to fantasy destinations
across an Earth as flat
as a map spread on the dining room table.

Our little legs are so short
they have to move twice as fast
to go half as far as before,
so we are always running late,

and time dwindles from the symphonic sprawl
of a languid evening at the concert hall
to the wristwatch and the ring tone
and the terse excuse and hasty promise
in the traffic jam or subway at that precise moment
half an hour after you should have been there
and half an hour before you now say you will arrive.

No time to talk over drinks at the interval,

our attention is not invested in the intimate.

We can spare the time it takes to like a meme

and check our notifications.

That's the most we can manage.

Once we spoke in confidence

and made confessions to each other.

Now conversation is scandal and exposure,

and risk averse, we hide our hearts.

We have nothing to hold onto anymore

but nothing has moved out of reach.

We ourselves have shrunk and can no longer stretch

as far as we once did. All our grasping

has made our arms wither. Do you remember?

Do you remember when we shared experiences

rather than retweeted secondhand remarks?

When words joined us in joy and in pain,

rather than stabbed us and split us apart?

So now we remove our skulls, sew our lips shut,

boil ourselves in herbs to preserve our skin,

use a block of wood to fill our heads,

decorate ourselves with beads,

and put ourselves on display like trophies.

No man's land

In the end

what we had thought matters most,

even to the exclusion of all other considerations,

turns out not to matter at all.

What turns out to be important

is something we have completely overlooked

the entire time, and so

I'll meet you in the no man's land

between false equivalence and false dichotomy,

between all the mutually exclusive competing certainties,

and we'll spread our picnic by some crater,

paddle in waters we've muddied with fallacy,

while artilleries of argument

cough contradictions at each other over our heads,

our only audience the skeletons of those

caught stumbling through wire barbed with ambiguity

strewn over earth peppered with shrapnel-seeds of doubt,

their last grimace of conviction melted from their bony faces,

until the only truth left for them to witness

is a wren perched in their empty eye-sockets for a while,

and our irrelevant truce, while it lasts,

before this permanent warfare intrudes upon our pleasantries,

shall be all the world knows of peace.

We'll talk about the ethics we only discover

once we run out of other excuses, not the morality

we use to express ideas of compassion

and understanding and responsibility,

but that sense of obligation that remains

even when we don't understand, have no clue, feel no pity,

but from which we draw meaning nevertheless,

because the alternative to credo is chaos,

and so we discuss how to stay loyal to the unknowable,

follow rival codes to conceal our common ignorance,

blame each other for their ambiguities,

and chase tattered banners across contested battlefields,

rather than confess, humbly, that we cannot explain our cause

any more than a shadow can describe the Sun.

Here in no man's land we find what we need without seeking it.

We find it in each other.

The courage to confess comes as a surprise.

We are most fortunate in our misfortune.

Digging[6]

Digging through dread, not digging in hope,

not anymore, you've been digging too long,

not knowing how long you have to dig,

you dig knowing already the only thing

that will bring your digging to an end,

the only reward waiting for you under the mud,

will be to take into your arms at last

something that until now only existed

in an imagination darker than the deepest pit,

born, made real, beneath the fallen mountain,

two hours before half term was due to start.

---

[6] Written on the 55th anniversary of the Aberfan disaster

The feast

Enjoy! This crisis is a feast,

an opportune disaster prepared

in the kitchen of our history.

Our host pillaged the forest

to lay this plunder on the table.

The hall is lit by sunsets summoned

from the veins of long dead beasts

and conjured into midnight candles.

We drink wine pressed from grapes

plucked from the vine before it burned.

Tree roots and the arteries of animals

tangle like a bed of noodles on the plate,

and there, on top, still beating,

pumping blood black oil to dress the rest,

the heart extracted from your empty chest.

Eat, for there is nothing left to grow.

This is the last food ever. Enjoy!

No score draw

Imagine, if you will, rather than a debate, a game.

There is a question we need to answer.

Something is being disputed, whether we like it or not.

We are seeking an outcome, a decision, a judgement,

so let's frame the process we've undertaken as a game,

with a winner and a loser, eventually, in theory, except:

1) There are no rules, at least, none that everyone agrees on.

2) Anyone can join any team as and when they feel like it,

swap sides, step aside, give up, change their mind,

join in again, and follow different rules to everyone else.

You can't choose who's on your side or how they play the game.

3) There is no normal play, only unlimited extra time,

during which the final whistle is blown continuously,

which can be a real headache, hence all the booze and drugs.

4) Multiple games must be played simultaneously,

on the same pitch but towards opposite ends.

5) Each team is considered collectively responsible
for all fouls committed by any individual member,
even if you refuse to recognise them as a teammate.

6) Reality is what the commentators say happened,
not what actually happened. There is always an angle
where the replay contradicts what you thought occurred,
which can then be discussed at length on radio phone-ins
where every fool airs every fallacy.

7) Appeals are not made to a referee - there is none -
but to motive, probability, analogy, consequence,
as whole teams of straw men "play the man,"
a game otherwise known as "ad hominem,"
and words themselves become footballs,
their meaning dependent on who is in possession.

8) Only own goals are counted when keeping score.

Everybody knows that everyone is wrong.
The mirage of a rule may emerge, evanescent,
against the run of play, from a sequence of passes,
but ultimately it will succumb to entropy,

as the move breaks down. Only advantage remains,

Nothing is ever settled, everything is at stake,

and no-one takes any prisoners, except, perhaps,

during a Christmas truce, once, in no-man's land,

when a real game was played in the interstice

that opened up briefly between the lines.

So how should we then play this game?

Should we be angels

as Aquinas describes them: deaf-blind people

walking through a world that they memorised

before the deity they obey rewound the tape,

seeming graceful among the chaos in playback

as they avoid the tackles,

looking like they were right all along?

Should we be demons

playing to galleries of sin in a whirlwind stadium

where the terraces are the eyewall of a storm

that slides across and slowly devastates the Earth,

happy to be wrong if they can take everyone else

down with them?

Or should we give each linesman a white flag to wave,

offer our surrender for all to see, though none will accept,

and spread our picnic on the centre spot,

to enjoy the spectacle of a no score draw.

Cabbage

Perhaps it's too late.
The rot has become
the load bearing part
of the structure.

Corruption is built in,
crime systemic,
apathy the default,
ignorance cultivated
and outrage reserved
for the expression
of prejudice.

The state is held hostage
by an almost imperceptibly
slow motion coup.
Democracy is the ruin
of a cabbage
after an evening of slugs.

We need to start again.

We need to plant seeds

and create conditions

for them to grow.

The hunt

They haven't got round to you yet.

They will eventually, like all the rest.

You think you're different? You're just the same.

It's just a matter of time

until it's you they find

when they're looking for someone to blame.

We're all illegal. We're all fugitives.

Don't confuse respite for safety,

even if you've enjoyed it your whole life.

The books will burn

and it'll be your turn.

They'll knock on your door one night,

because rules are all unwritten,

though they drift on and off the page,

and even though you think you're in charge

the dogs will turn on you one day.

The wrack

We idealise our fellow passengers

because reality is too painful to consider.

We forget the cruelty, absolve the sadism,

so casual, so relaxed, so unremarkable

that it is not remarked upon.

We disregard the teeth bared in every smile,

the snarl in every laugh.

We approach the subject in a controlled manner,

crop and collimate it in the aperture of our words,

and manipulate it into an acceptable form

with the molten, malleable lens of our sentences.

Polite lexicons inventorise

the locked archive of our imperial mischief,

the derelict war museum of the mind.

We are drowned citizens of sunken cities,

the sea surrounding us an amniosis of amnesia.

Crabs escape their ruined ribcage creels

in the barnacled marketplace.

Statues personifying virtues we extolled,

gestures frozen in a paralysis of hypocrisy,

marble faces clenched in a rictus of righteousness

as they clinch some pointless argument,

wear the kelp laurel of futility's triumph,

monuments to the broken compromise

between competing cruelties above the waves.

We slip past mines and sink to this place,

following our anchor to the seabed,

any grip on the world above purchased

only by loosening someone else's fingers first.

The storm gives expression to a rage we deny,

an anger of unknown origin that will never be satisfied

and consumes our vessel. We abandon ship,

abandon each other, abandon ourselves:

the individual is what remains of every doomed collective

after their successive disintegrations;

the sinking ship, the lifeboat overwhelmed by the swell,

the flotsam and uncertain fate to which we cling,

hope bought with coin minted from the despair

of those left for dead at every increment of disaster

until at last we each drown alone in useless wealth

and all that is left to do before we go is ask our children

to forgive us for the fragments of humanity they inherit.

An astronomer in Ukraine[7]

The astronomer descends from the observatory to the street.

Stars are siphoned by her telescope into a silicon net. Caught,

displayed and studied, their ancient light, their long cold heat,

the fingerprint of their spectra, the exoplanet's swagger, the beat

and slow sway of its waltz with its companion: her thoughts

turn from here to worlds where perhaps things thought unique

once, divine blessings bestowed with complicated benevolence,

gifts from God with strings attached that later act as precedent

and prototype for the more worldly forms of puppetry

attempted by those who think strength confers authority,

turn out to be a cosmic commonplace, miracles on repeat,

and she descends from her observatory to the street,

exchanging precision optics unblemished by the merest speck

of dust for a dirty old bottle, filled with fuel, rag in its neck,

fuel formed from a miracle of life on which our sun once shone

and as that ancient heat and light is released

it helps bring about an earthly dictator's defeat.

---

[7] Written after reading about an astronomer describing how she had to divide her time between her studies and making Molotov cocktails.

Christchurch

Tell us the names of the victims.

Let the names of those who killed them

already be forgotten.

Let the victims' names live forever.

Tell us how they lived and loved. Today.

when words are most difficult

but most necessary, use them

to tell us about the gardens they kept.

the books they read and reread.

Tell us about the games they loved to play.

the subjects that inspired them to study.

their ambitions, their charity, their piety,

that saw them kneel where they were shot,

to pray to God with their last thought.

Make a book with pages of silk,

bound in gold, to record this for the ages.

and save a page for me. Save a page

for all of us, but do not spare a single word,

do no commit a single stroke of your pen

to write the names of those who did this.

Let their names be forgotten.

Rebel

All rebels are rebels without a cause.

They thought they had a cause once,

but times change. It becomes more of a pretext,

an excuse, a vague, nebulous sense of discontent.

Yes, the world's broken,

but although we start off by thinking we can bridge

the great chasm running down the middle of things,

eventually we realise it runs through the middle of us,

and our revolution stalls, dwindles and thins out

until it becomes an ideological comb over,

a story we tell ourselves to pretend we are still young,

a reflection we turn towards to see our good side,

the precarious arrangement of mirrors we prop up

to observe ourselves side on, in heroic profile,

then curse the double chin that ruins it.

When we were young, we practised our microphone pose,

imagining crowds rallied by our incandescent truth.

Now we grow old, and our powers wane, and we realise

we have failed to deliver our youthful insights in time,

before it dawned on us that we were wrong about everything.

We are betrayed by every hero, one by one, until at last

we are betrayed by ourselves. History does not remember

those who deserve the credit, only those who claim it,

and the only progress that we recognise and celebrate

is eventually revealed to be fraudulent anyway.

To make a difference, first accept obscurity,

and whatever revolution there is in that

will be known only to you.

Cuff links

There was an election today.

I wore my special voting cuff links,
the small round black ones,
suitable to wear with formal evening attire,

because elections here are black tie affairs,
and voting is very formal and prestigious,
an elegant evening reception. "Why hello,"
I remark to my neighbour, "aren't the booths
and their various accoutrements appointed
in the most delightful manner this year?"

There is a real sense of democratic occasion,
a promenade of civic pride: "democracy
- the most exclusive club in town,
except everyone's invited". You get
a complimentary prosecco after you cast your vote.

Hors d'oeuvre are provided in the gym hall,

where tea is served in bone china cups and saucers,

and sipped, pinkies out, between pleasantries.

People are wearing silk scarves and satin lapels.

And oh! Everyone is so polite! The civility!

"I voted Nazi, what about you?"

"Oh, it's communist for me, all the way."

"You rogue." And eventually

the conversation turns to the weather.

Rio Grande[8]

Not Styx, not Lethe, not Cocytus,

but the Rio Grande:

which circle of Hell lies this side

of our southern border?

The little girl and her father

didn't make it across to us,

but their failure carried us over

to the other side of Acheron.

---

[8] Prompted by the distressing scene of Óscar Alberto Martínez Ramírez and his 23-month-old daughter, Valeria, who drowned trying to cross the Rio Grande river from Mexico to the USA.

Lungs

The Aegean[9].

The Rio Grande.

Water in a child's lungs,

like two tear shaped sacks.

I would cry,

but my eyes are as dry

as deserts fled by refugees

when the climate trespasses

upon their crops,

in this age of dust bowl and deluge.

We weep with our lungs now

and grieve for our own extinction

with the bodies of dead children.

---

[9] The beach near Bodrum, Turkey, where the body of Alan Kurdi was recovered.

Vox pop

"Send them back. You know what I mean?

That's just my opinion, but they come over here,

get all the houses, all the doctor's appointments,

all the school places. That's just what I heard.

"They're benefit scroungers, claiming asylum,

and they work all the hours God sends

to put their kids through uni. Doctors and lawyers."

[I hate myself, and it's all their fault,

and somebody else's problem,

you know what I mean?

Please tell me you know what I mean!]

"Someone should do something. That's just my opinion.

They're all paedophiles, aren't they?

That's just what I heard. You know what I mean?

That's just my opinion."

[I can't be bothered finding anything out for myself

or thinking anything through

so, my toxic ignorance is now your problem,

and I will feign pride in what secretly disgusts me about myself

in order to force you to deal with it.]

"You know what I mean?

That's just my opinion."

Let Eton stand

"Floreat Etona"

- the motto of Eton College

Other edifices may burn down -

royal residences in Windsor,

tower blocks in North Kensington -

but let Eton stand, and flourish

for now. Let its playing fields

remain innocent and unmolested

by the trench and barbed wire of Flanders.

Let friendly bombs fall somewhere else

a few miles to the north, on Slough,

while old boys address us on the radio,

with whimsical contempt: "floreat Etona[10]

et flagret Grenfell," their polite words

lending fragrance to miasmas of privilege

that stifle all other voices like mustard gas,

or smoke in burning tower blocks, smiling

---

[10] Prompted by a particularly obnoxious interview I heard on BBC Radio 4 with Jacob Rees-Mogg. He didn't say "flagret Grenfell" but I felt it was implied.

as they strangle us with their subjunctives

and murder us with their "common sense".

So, let Eton stand, its halls intact, not in ruins,

not as some mystery to invite speculation

like the works of Ozymandias,

but to remind us always of what it stood for:

six centuries perverting education

into a weapon of class war,

making a privilege of what should be a right

for all who can benefit from it.

You say tear Eton down.

Let Eton stand. Let it fall

only into discredited dilapidation.

Let it rest like a derelict wreck

upon the bank of a civil discourse

that flows past its decaying edifice,

its walls a warning, environs haunted,

precincts shunned by the very children

whose minds it once poisoned

because of the monsters lurking there.

Station

In the immaculate solitude,

> steam rising through the light into the soft night rain,

> the Solari board chatter mesmerising the obedient mob,

> who populate this perfect absence,

> distracted by pleasant fictions of origin and arrival,

> destination and departure, route and return,

> living their impossible timetabled lives

> beguiled by myths of choice and liberty,

> believing themselves co-conspirators

> in the reckless velocity of civilisation,

> while remaining all equally alien, unknown and apart,

> empty static separated shapes in this step-swept space,

> their dreams invaded and hollowed out by the pulse,

> fluorescent flicker and flat-chested billboard pout,

> of the city's robotic sexuality,

> leaving only a place in time and space

> an outline through which a stranger passes,

> a silhouette en route to a sepulchre,

I marvel at the secret revelry,

the private pageant, of my loneliness:

> a little snail ekes out its tallow path

alone on the polished floor,

a devil-kissed discard, companion of dust,

propelled by the blinding slow-motion spasm

the ridiculous lifelong convulsion

of the single long slow sneeze,

with which it mutely heaves itself through its life,

through the high dark brightness of my mind,

tense, suspended in agony, the freeze frame

of an unending angelic bellyflop,

of a perverted, inverted keel-haul across the floor

that encompasses everything it will ever know,

every path it will ever take in the few hours it lives,

and as the hectic eclectic collection of strangers pass,

curtsey, bow, and polka to the platform,

in the movies of their own lives playing in their minds

carrying their hopes and dreams to unknowable futures

neatly wrapped in individual billboard boxes,

imagined lives garlanded with fantasy,

I must remember where I am:

I am here, now. For in that thought

I receive the announcement of love

broadcast from all other isolations,

from the destinations the Solari cannot articulate:

palaces and torture chambers,

spotlights and space flights, wombs and tombs,

from every coffin inhabited by memory,

every cavity that has felt the draft of our passing,

and from those souls set free by misfortune:

born limbless and snail blind,

imbecile tongues tied and torsos twisted,

whom we weep with joy to behold

for their inviolable innocence,

the nutshell and infinite space

of their impenetrable imprisoned imaginations,

the garbled Morse of their transmissions,

their orbits awkward, stumbling, retrograde,

mysterious and indecipherable to us

as the whispered pizzicato

of the gentle night rain on the skylight,

and just because we can't understand

does not mean they are not speaking

and we love them,

sore for what we cannot know.

I must remember in case I am left crying other tears,

the hard and arid tombstone tears of Lina Kretschmar[11]

    letting grief for the wreckage of false gods

    tumbling from her womb

    outweigh love for the broken child,

    seething caustic tears slowly sucking dry the whole earth

    with withering ripples of desiccation girding the place

    where she drops her round stone squealing farrow

    from her eye, tears kilned and immured

    in hollow hearts, subterranean tears,

    burrowing and burying themselves

    like eager brick seeds

    that bring forth chimneys at the terminus

    stiff slender stems with steel rail roots

    that blossom with ash

    billows filling and stilling the thickening night,

    enough ash to clog every pore,

    smother every duct of feeling,

    until memories are dark shapes in the strata,

    shadows where the flesh had been,

    swift puffs of powder people

    passing through the perfect absence

---

[11] Mother of Gerhard Kretschmar, first victim of the policy that would become known as Aktion T-4.

in this dreadful night that has no mother,

this empty mother-shaped night of abandonment,

this black-hot lead-lined box of dread that dumps

its uneven weight upon the scales of equinox,

tips the world's unruly embers into pits of melancholy,

then pours its molten self away

as stinking tears sinking to fill the deep dark toxic aquifer of fire

that brims beneath this city and fuels us still

and burns every word I utter

the instant my tongue prints it into speech,

and flashes my tears to steam

rising through the rain,

to be lost with yours in the clouds,

the clouds beyond the night sky

that dissolve our tears,

where we relax at last our grip on pain,

which we search through

and illuminate with love,

and where we must finally lose ourselves

to be together with each other again,

so quickly take this tongue-pressed ticket to my heart

while I'm still here

and make the connection.

Stowaway[12]

What should we do now?

Do our acts of remembrance

merely complete our amnesia?

At one and the same time

as we remember what we know was lost

do we erase what has been forgotten

in the rituals of commemoration?

We only make room on our monuments

for the names we remember.

Does memory also include the possibility,

at least, of what cannot be remembered?

At the memorial for what we lost,

the order of service, the list of the lost,

is a manifest that ignores the stowaways,

disregards the unregistered and illegal,

articulates what is a matter of record only

and, as it must, leaves what is unsayable

unsaid: on one hand we briefly touch

our outstretched fingertips to our friend's

---

[12] Written on the occasion of Holocaust Memorial Day 2015

as they fall forever out of reach; on the other,

we didn't even know that they existed,

so perfect is their annihilation.

What other Adams crumbled back to dust

while God's Sistine digit reached out to us,

and in the end failed to stop even our fall?

But weren't we all stowaways once?

Rather than just remember

what must not be forgotten

– floral tributes solemnly laid

on the tops of stone monuments –

perhaps we should not forget to mourn

the incalculable loss

of what cannot now be remembered.

Unseal the tomb. See

that all we share with its occupant

who stood next to us on previous occasions

is an emptiness that we can crawl inside

to curl up in alone, hiding

in the borrowed shadows of their sepulchre

on our own private journey

in the vessel it makes for us.

The waters we are embarked upon

are dark and unforgiving, grief strewn,

and in the inevitable end

we don't know who else clings

to the wreckage in the night,

or who has succumbed already to the cold

to sink at last into their pit of private terror

without a trace, without ever being known,

without even having the chance of being remembered.

The light of day does not reveal the depths,

it only reveals the debris, only the jetsam

around which we locked our rigid fingers,

as we turned ourselves into objects to survive,

the debris from which we now make

our grim reckoning of loss,

and delude ourselves that we are better prepared

for the next storm,

for it is only in the limitless, inaccessible depths,

where the sunken bodies eventually come to rest,

that the truth is known.

So let us not just commemorate

what we know of our loss.

Let us remember

that we will never know its full extent.

Let us not pretend

we are prepared for the future,

all epaulettes and medals

mumbling pious voodoo at the helm.

Let us now think about

those now living that we overlook today,

and render assistance

to the refugee and to the stowaway,

no matter who they are

or where they're from or what they flee

and fill up to overflowing

now our empty memory

as the only way to make up

for what was lost without a trace.

The innocents[13]

Surely God must be there somewhere?

In the quiet midday rubble?

So many children killed

weren't killed for no reason?

It must be because God was among them?

Surely the endless daily routine of pain

and fear and loss and grief and dusty pallor

that suffocates and erases their childhood

is because our rulers heard a rumour somewhere?

Surely shrapnel pierces limbs

and phosphorus burns flesh

and rubble is heaped upon bodies

because our rulers have somewhere heard a rumour,

have a dossier somewhere that describes in detail,

that God is somehow, somewhere among them,

as Herod found out, long ago,

and are exhausting the sum of Man's futile strength,

calling in every air-strike, dropping every bomb,

---

[13] Written in response to the bombardment of civilian populations in Syria

in jealousy and rage against Him

while we sit safe at home bathed in TV light,

entertained by the tedious percussion of foreign wars?

Is God now a refugee?

Following weary parents

on the long low road to foreign lands

to be greeted with suspicion and denigration

as happened long ago in Bethlehem and Egypt?

Do we turn God away at Yarmouk and Calais?

Do we spit on God and call Him names?

Or have we managed to kill God at last,

relentlessly pursuing Herod's mission to completion,

leaving us with nothing but dead children?

Have we now become the angel of death,

no longer following some divine plan,

not passing over, but unconstrained

except by earthly dictates, flexing air-forces

in ineffective, indiscriminate, macho gestures?

Surely God must be there somewhere?

Please let God be there somewhere.

The experiment[14]

We created it in the desert, from human debris

that survived the chaos of our last war:

scattered body parts assembled, stitched together

and brought to life with the accumulated trauma

of a million dumbstruck orphans.

It stumbled at first, a stranger to its own limbs.

We propped it up. Our allies bound its wounds.

We indulged its simple appetite for atrocity,

buying its plunder, plying it with more bullets.

Priests well-versed in hate taught it to speak.

We directed its primitive sectarian urges

against dictators who did not yet toe our line.

We tell the world we are blending new poisons

to make a final cure for an old disease,

as if that makes any sense at all.

When the medicine we concoct boils over

and briefly spills and sizzles on the hob,

---

[14] For example, ISIS emerged from the jails in which prisoners captured by the allies in Iraq were kept.

we sprinkle more bombs into our alchemy,

and distil more profits from the blood.

War aims narrow to a cycle of retaliation.

Friends and enemies are rendered interchangeable

by every outrage. Ghostly children

emerge from ruins, pale with dust,

to find out whose side they are on now,

and another generation of human wreckage

is strewn across the sand, ready

for the next time we need to make a monster.

The song of the arms dealers

We stuffed our coffers fast and full

while workers filled their coffins.

We piled our profits rafter-high

and left them just one option:

to take a single King's shilling

and to make their children orphans,

and gave to them thanks of a grateful nation.

Year after year, war after war,

we sold the guns they'd need.

We sold the bombs and kept no scores,

whatever made them bleed.

He sold them his, I sold them mine,

we'd toast how well we'd done,

and gave to them thanks of a grateful nation.

No mustard gas in St Tropez,

no mistral at Verdun,

no justice bought for any price

while we controlled the coin,

and French and German coughed their last

while we were having fun,

and giving them thanks of a grateful nation.

It wasn't champagne in our glass,

it wasn't crystal chiming,

it wasn't fine wine that we drank

while dancing and fine dining.

but workers blood in workers skulls,

while workers did the dying,

and got from us thanks of a grateful nation.

And you sleep soundly in your bed.

You do not drown in mud

beneath a flare and flack filled sky

amid the screams and thuds.

You do not really wonder why.

You do not ask. Instead

you give to them thanks of a grateful nation.

The monastery

Although these monks practised every vice to its extreme,

their virtue somehow remained intact,

as though there was some obscure higher purpose,

some forensic detachment, or aloofness of demeanour,

that mitigated their every trespass. Every foray into this world

every observance of its ways and customs, every degradation,

was somehow clandestine, a subterfuge, all evils necessary

so that the saint could infiltrate the world undiscovered,

and become familiar with our turpitude under cover of sin.

Obscenity and innocence were interchangeable,

both equally stratagems of this same high mission.

Moral considerations were mere cards to be played

for stakes that were never made clear to us

according to rules that changed with every hand.

The monks did not compromise their vows

when they cast off their habit and dressed like us,

talked with us, adopted our loud profanities,

joined in our revels, belched, raised a glass with us

in blasphemous praise of undeserving sinners

and their gross, prodigious exploits, their notoriety,

their transient moment upon the crucifix of fame

and their well-publicised parodies of glory,

or remained silent, like us, in church, when praise was due,

surreptitiously pilfering alms from the collection plate as it passed

to squander on unsanctified wine in some less holy place

where we raised cathedrals of flesh, and demolished them,

and reclined among their ruins mocking all reputation,

luxuriating in the wreckage of our renown,

and made the altars anvils of our lust. Their rule was a riddle

beyond the comprehension of all wit, so it was said.

The inscrutable will of God was no mere premise

to be elaborated by human reason limping in pursuit

in the lame logical progression of the rule's ordinances.

Rather, the rule itself defied scrutiny, embodied that will,

so it was said (for those who had read it were all now mad),

and so the monks it ruled were tolerated on the basis of faith alone

and their every whim and excess and transgression indulged

because of an equivalence with virtue

reckoned in some lost algebra

by which they led us step by step towards an understanding

we would eventually come to regret more than anything else.

and we ordained them with our own eagerness

to believe in an impossible salvation.

We came to realise our own footsteps marked out their cloister

in every shadow-swept alley

where souls are traded for expediency. for brief neon vanities

and temporary respite from self-inflicted pain.

and as our options narrowed with every poor decision.

as our desire for the numbing anaesthesia of lust or revenge abated

- the cycle of vengeance itself exhausted us.

and we tired of each other's gradually declining bodies -

as our appetites became dull

through over-indulgence and familiarity and fatigue.

and our own decline instructed us in matters of priority.

as we found we had to be selective

about where we invested our energy.

we gradually recognised in the acquiescence.

the tolerance and reconciliation that became the only things

for which we could any longer summon up the effort.

not redemption. no, not redemption.

but an uncanny resemblance to redemption

that was the cruellest possible condemnation,

the deceptive verisimilitude of virtue,

a redemption we would now forever be denied,

the apparent virtue of a condition

to which we had condemned ourselves,

the easy virtue of depleted sin

for which we could never claim any credit

and which we could no longer escape with any extravagance of vice.

The monks departed,

abandoning us to a monastery of our own making,

where we were imprisoned without reprieve,

and we found all we had to hold on to was each other

and the desire to deliver ourselves was thwarted

by the addict's inability to accept grace undefiled,

but to pay a price for everything.

Human

Maybe we aren't human after all.

Maybe we are wild animals pretending to be human,

and society is our habitat, where we are lost in mimicry,

prowling through a jungle of replicated behaviours,

and the person we think we are is an elaborate copy of our prey,

a disguise we adopt to avoid startling it as we close in,

and our perseverance in its pursuit has been so thorough

we have forgotten that's all it is,

and we lure ourselves into traps we set for others,

and as we fall into them

our futile protest echoes within the mirror's deceit.

Maybe we aren't human after all, and our words are redundant,

as noises free of their semantic burden would suffice:

simple territorial declarations, mating calls,

intimate tautologies reiterated as acts of grooming,

tiny gestures of supplication and social cohesion;

or perhaps distant, mysterious, remote cries of distress or ecstasy,

heard at midnight, which we are never sure we heard correctly

and which are never heard again to let us decide which.

That line between repetition and ambiguity,

that boundary between tautology and silence,

between light and dark, is:

a tightrope we try to walk

in the brief intoxicated span and spasm of a poem

before stumbling off into the margins

to wander back to the bone-crushing loneliness of night, or;

a tripwire we discover with a reckless remark

that ends a relationship, or;

a throat cut at midnight

from which we drink warm dark blood

before retreating into the shadows to be at one again

with the ageless, nameless, incomprehensible evil

that provoked that cry of ecstasy or distress

before it was swiftly curtailed, or;

a rope with which we tie a noose around the Moon,

turning astronomy into an inverted execution,

planets balloon worlds tethered to our imagination of mud,

dangling inert, upside down, warning the stars to avoid this place,

because maybe we are not human after all.

Maybe we are just wild animals.

Tapestry

Reality is narrative. At least,

any reality that we can describe and share.

Beyond the fraying edge of our stories

there is a vast empty solitude

with which we each must make our individual peace,

and all our myths are littered with deals and trades,

forlorn bargains offered to the indifferent abyss.

It is the tales we tell

- to ourselves, to each other -

that turn this wilderness into a home.

We imbue the world with depth and duration

to make a space we can occupy together.

All the stars would be orphans,

peering through the threadbare sky,

without the constellations

into which we gather and arrange them.

Every sight is surface without our efforts

to fathom the meanings they might conceal.

We begin to remember once we begin to speak,

the bliss of infantile amnesia caught like a butterfly,

dried and pinned and labelled and put on display,

and we tell our story, and celebrate our induction

into the shared hallucination of humanity

as the thread of our story is woven with the rest,

and we bid farewell to the company we kept as an animal

among the trees and rocks and birds and beasts,

and the other diverse objects of delirious infancy:

an alternate reality that can now only intrude dreamlike,

- familiar yet half-remembered -

into the common dream we now call reality,

as seldom as unicorns and hippogriffs,

to populate the tales we tell on those rarest of occasions

when we want to share something intimate of ourselves

among the pageant of hope and memory.

Active shooter

It is a remarkable achievement:

writing about that

about which it is impossible to write,

saying that which is impossible to say,

the interruption of our unreality,

that personality our brain invents

to explain its own existence to itself,

the depopulation of our imagined world,

and the replacement of words with bullets,

and every second made suddenly heavy

with the weight of one more future unbegun,

like the weight of a tombstone on the tongue.

It is a poem written by removing words,

not by adding them. Breath is held, locked down,

in a hiding place, while names disappear

from the school register, one by one.

It is a remarkable, terrible achievement,

this lead redaction, chambered and hoarsely sung

by a gunmetal throat into a silent world.

Seven balloons at sunset

Eating raw peppers like apples
on my balcony in Vilnius,
- big, juicy, bulbous red peppers -
we watch the evening cavalcade
of balloons floating slowly past.
The sun sets, but hot air rises
and with each bite we see,
in the twilight, the most magnificent
monuments of nonchalance.

They float through the cool evening air,
replacing the tyranny of temperature
that had seized the hot May midday
by the throat, for no good reason
but to deny enjoyment of the sun
while shadows still exist.

So, in the cool evening air,

the balloons float past the TV tower

where the martyrs died[15]

one cold day in January,

and without even noticing

they drift over the border fence

between today and tomorrow,

and the peppers taste good.

---

[15] 14 unarmed civilians lost their lives and 700 were injured opposing the Soviet military seizure of the tower on 13 January 1991

The rain[16]

The rain fell

half a day too late,

the difference

between falling on fire

and falling on ash.

Twelve hours earlier

we would have blessed this rain.

Now it may as well

never fall again.

---

[16] Written the morning after the June 2018 Glasgow School of Art Fire

August 6th, 1945

A new way of seeing needs new eyes.

Our old ones must vacate their sockets[17]

and surrender them to this new light

that fills them all with brief and bright

irradiance from a single burning bulb

for a fraction of a second and forever.

Some call this way of seeing blindness.

I see the blind gather by the river[18]

to rinse the old world from their eyes,

its old light thickening with ash

and time itself a twisted wreck

on which upheaval drapes itself.

---

[17] "their faces were wholly burned, their eye sockets were hollow, the fluid from their melted eyes had run down their cheeks" (John Hersey, "The New Yorker" magazine, 31 August 1946)

[18] "Hiroshima was laced by seven tributaries of the Ota River. Survivors ran to the rivers with skin hanging off the in shreds, moaning 'Mizu, mizu!' (Water, water)" (Marcel Junod)

Our eyes now hood a common candle

carried in their separate sockets

to shed and share that self-same light.

for there is now only a single sight

to see. all things collapsing into one

beneath a sudden. unforgiving sun.

Secondary target

It should have been Kokura,

not us. But for clouds and cockups,

it would have been Kokura.

And after the bomber diverted to Okinawa

because the reserve tank pump had failed

and it wouldn't make it back to Tinian

and the engines cut out on landing

due to fuel exhaustion,

the newspapers even got its name wrong:

it was the Bockscar, not the Great Artiste;

and its target was Nagasaki, not Kokura.

August 9th, 1945

The sky inhaled the earth today.

At 11am the cloudy Kyushu sky

breathed in. It sucked the earth up

through a long sore smoky throat

into a lung of fire,

and when it finally breathed out

it raised the city up on its palm

and pursed its lips

and blew away the ashes of our bones.

Caesium 137

I remember when I first met you:
1988, Glasgow, an undergraduate lab class,
a flask of radioactive mud taken from the drains
in the aftermath of Chernobyl, two years before.

We were suitably cautioned and handled you with care
lest you infiltrate bone, settle in marrow,
decay by emitting gene-shredding electrons
that announce your presence with leukaemia
and leave a residue of barium[19] in rib and femur,
a stable daughter lying undisturbed for centuries,
your signature enduring in a premature grave
for future archaeologists to interpret,

but you entered my life before that:
in the rain that fell that day in April 1986,
and in the grass that fed the sheep
and cooked them from the inside just enough
to have them taken by the million from the hills
before they could end up on our tables.

---

[19] ^{137}Cs decays to ^{137m}Ba by β-emission, which decays to ^{137}Ba by γ-emission.

but even before that you were there,

a minute residue of Hiroshima, a trace, a stratum,

dividing all human history into two eras:

the Pre-caesium-137 Age and the Post,

your absence in old claret a proof of pre-war vintage.

because we'd have to go back aeons,

long before grapes grew in the chalky soils of St Emilion,

long before the beguiling balance of risk and reward

tempting organisms to explore their surroundings

teased life into the phylogenetic diversity we see around us

that first erupted in the Cambrian Explosion,

before single cells first embraced as gametes,

ending billions of generations of loneliness,

to find you in the cloud of detritus and rubble

from which the Earth was formed,

dwindling away after the concatenation of half lives

that had elapsed since you were first born

in the collision of neutron stars that bequeathed to us

the uranium we unravel today to heat our homes,

and destroy the armies of our enemies,

and confer on you a second birth

that buries us in your resurrection.

There is no justice

There is no justice.
When the right things happen
it's for the wrong reasons
and the wrong things happen
all the time anyway.

The appearance of justice
is an illusion,
a temporary alignment
without real significance,
a coincidence, like that one day
your horoscope came true.

When you read in the paper
"justice was served"
it just means someone
had the good fortune to get
what they were looking for,
and someone else
got paid to write about it
for whatever reason.

There is no justice,

and the rich get rich,

and the children starve,

while a jury of celebrities

says which of them got talent

and a parliament of Tories

says none of them get food.

Justice is the smoke

they blow up your arse

while they leave you broke.

Justice is what they call

the rules that they break

and the news that they fake

while they're on the take

and they take it all.

That's what they call it.

Justice. There is no justice.

The state of Denmark

What do you mean, "something
rotten in the state of Denmark"?
There is always something rotten
in the state of Denmark,
always has been and always will be.

Your statement is a tautology.
Things are pristine and vivid
only in the imagination.
Reality is a still born whelp.
You prod it with a stick
expecting it to flinch
and instead, it bursts open
and spews out all that feeds on it,
whole parliaments of maggots,
and you act surprised?
The state is a carcass
whose procedures are decay.

Gestating better worlds in the mind

as we patrol the hard border

between possibility and disappointment

is a job that will never be complete.

The ravine

We shout abuse

at each other

across the ravine.

It fills with bodies

for whom no-one speaks.

From cliff edge we cast

words like quick lime

to cover the dead

and forget. At night

we tell our children stories

in which we are the heroes.

In the morning we give

our wives a doorstep kiss,

and leave, and return

to the ravine.

Day after day,

shoulder to shoulder,

forgiving our brothers,

condemning all others,

we hate and we love

and the bodies float past.

The fragment

The fragment read: "What if

no-one agrees with each other?

What if we only think we do,

but were we truly to understand

each other's reasons and motivations

we would be utterly horrified?

"What if we are all monsters,

cannibals on our best behaviour,

and civilisation is cutlery and cross-purpose,

"a teetering, unstable scaffold

of mutually supportive mistakes,

upon which we climb to announce

opinions to no-one, everyone nodding

agreeing without knowing or understanding

what they are agreeing to,

the impression of agreement

just one big happy coincidence?

"Forget those who disagree with you.

You know where they stand better

than those with whom you agree.

The danger is behind you, not facing you.

Hate seeks cover in virtuous accord.

What envenomed fragrance we breathe

in the perfumed arguments of our allies?

Chaos finds camouflage in reason.

"Logic is an artefact of saying things

one at a time rather than all at once.

It places them in order so the world

will fit the sleeve of speech,

"but were we to see behind its façade,

and see all at once everything it conceals,

we'd see it hides the stampede

of who we truly are,

a beast of ecstasies and atrocities

that feigns domestication

for a loaf of daily bread

from the temple granary."

It took generations of scholarship

to reassemble the broken tablets,

decipher the cuneiform, and only then

discover we had retrieved a partial text,

one side of a conversation in a lost epic,

a dispute between kings and gods

in the ruined city's foundation myth.

The god's reply is a matter

of academic speculation.

The disaster circus

Everything that can be said
has already been said. All variations
on the theme have been explored,
and we now just endlessly recapitulate
that we are simply begging for our lives.

The last ringmaster hangs
from the top pole
with the trapeze for a noose.
The big top is a tumbril,
and with blood for greasepaint,
clowns control the disaster circus,
juggling excuses in the soiled sawdust,
giving their tedious, exhausting display
of malignant surrealism
to a captive audience,
mistaking our cries for applause
as we beg for our lives,
and performing more atrocities
in response,

so do not beg.

Fight back. The flip side of futility

is perseverance despite it all,

meeting death's grimace with disdain

which no loss can defeat. Fight back,

and one day you will recognise victory

from her fragility, and cherish her

for as long as you

are left in peace to do so.

We knew this day was coming

We knew the day was coming,
the day that we had feared,
but found we had done nothing
to prepare once it was here.

At first they cut our tongues out
then demanded that we speak
and laughed at how we mumbled
when our mouths could only bleed.

They ground our bones for baking
the bread that they would serve
to the midget in his bunker
in a tale turned on its head.

They rewound modern history
like it was old videotape
and made us watch the classics,
an atrocity hit parade.

We learned to be grateful

as a way to stay alive

now the calculus of victory

is merely managing to survive.

We knew this day was coming,

the day that we have feared,

but find we have done nothing

to prepare now it is here.

The fallen statues[20]

What shall we place now on our empty plinths?

Or shall we leave them empty and vacant
to testify with eloquent silence
to new ambition, humble and benign,
yet greater than the fortunes of one man?

Then let us uncommemorate their crimes,
so ghosts of anonymous, unremembered victims
can step into the space, occupying the absence
from which we evacuate the monument,
and we can spend our time
imagining a future less malign.

---

[20] Following the toppling of the statue of slave trader Edward Colston in Bristol on 7 June 2020

Children's crusade

They say don't worry,

we all grow up.

These playground histrionics

where everything is staked

on a single petty disagreement

will abate, and one day

we'll all feel embarrassed by our conduct,

and learn good faith, respect, humility,

and how to live together in the twilight

between unanimity and annihilation.

They say that, but we won't.

We will defend our errors to the grave.

We will end up as old fools,

spitting ad hominem and tu quoque

and cui bono at each other,

deploying our straw armies

to hold entrenched positions,

identifying with the struggle

and missing the point.

We are all on a Children's Crusade,

all ultimately standing on the shore,

waiting for the Mediterranean to part

and grant us passage to the Holy Land,

and falling prey to every passing brigand

who would sell us into slavery

in the meantime.

The barbarians

We were so confident once. We believed

the righteous held the commanding heights.

Occasional expeditions against recalcitrant chaos

were sometimes required, but we were civilised

and our politics was a cavalcade of rationality.

We made art to celebrate our triumph.

We felt good about ourselves.

Now we are the outlaws,

cowering in some mountain refuge,

and the barbarians sit where once we made laws,

declaring their passing whims

equivalent to our most solemn deliberations

and toppling our monuments for sport,

but remember: they will not remain;

we don't have to become like them;

we must never become like them.

Someday we'll raise our banner

over the ruins of everything we ever achieved

having driven the enemy away, a victory of sorts

in a war that should not have been fought.

Even in our moment of triumph we will know

lessons have not been learned,

and our victory is not final.

Victory does not vindicate the violence

with which it is purchased, it buys time,

creates a breathing space where we can talk

about doing things another way, for a while at least.

This barbarism was not new.

This barbarism was always there,

but we had grown so accustomed to its habits

we deferred to them, applauded even

those moments of finesse we called civilisation.

For all the corrupt advantage taken of the present,

the past had always been more brutal, but extenuated

by a recollection that must make peace with it.

And so, again, every common cause is subverted.

Doubts grow from whispers to shouts.

Every altruistic impulse is stalled by second guess,

and public space is surrendered to private security,

as we retreat behind the walls of our compound,

and safety becomes a gift bestowed by gangsters

to whom mock baronial privilege accrues in chaos.

Yet I will fasten my banner to the barrel of a gun

and raise it over a burning Reichstag once more,

and you will call it righteous

and do the same yourself someday.

The muttering undergrowth of Hamburg

I charge my wine to my room[21].

The staff ask me if it satisfactory.

I repeat some acceptable formula

to express my contentment.

The lobby pianist mangles

a series of reassuringly recognisable tunes:

standards, movie themes, nothing that risks

a genuinely emotional response.

No one expects too much,

but more than this,

more than what the undergrowth tells me,

the muttering undergrowth of Hamburg.

I go for a stroll by the Außenalster.

It's not fireflies in the bushes.

Cheap high brightness LEDs

pilfered from a market

illuminate that futile university

---

[21] Hotel Atlantic, Hamburg

among the soggy sleeping bags

from which we graduate in death.

The undergrowth mutters under its breath

as it reads to itself: Goethe, Sartre,

or some ghost-written celebrity bio,

whatever could be lifted easily

from the library, or the discount bookstore

where remaindered stock is sold,

but not to them,

not to these remaindered people:

their currency is theft

backed by the bank of midnight death.

I can't see faces. The undergrowth

becomes suddenly aware of my presence,

and falls silent, then an arm is thrust out,

and another, and another,

and a hollow howling hopeless plea is made,

wilting with generations of disappointment,

begging me in a thousand languages I don't understand,

but I understand perfectly what they say,

and they describe me perfectly

when I walk away.

I charge my wine to my room.

The staff ask me if it satisfactory.

I repeat some acceptable formula

to express my contentment.

Victory

Enjoy victory while it lasts,
so the memory gives you strength
when next you need it.

The inner scream is reduced
to a whisper for a while. Remember
when tumult next surrounds you.

Perhaps all we ever win is memory,
a reason to keep fighting
the next time that we lose.

Celebrate. Drink all the drinks.
Dance and kiss your comrades,
for there are no victories,

only varying degrees of defeat, shuffled,
dealt, gathered in, and shuffled once again.
What we call victory is relative and temporary.

so love, laugh, and keep living,

until you can no longer

outlive your enemies.

Election day

Dogs on pedestals bark at each other.

We tell ourselves stories to persuade ourselves
that what we tolerate is indeed tolerable.

The landfill reeks. The city is a scaffold
made from the bones of industries milked dry,
stripped bare, and abandoned to obsolescence
so that the rich may keep their treasure.

There once was a chapel where Teneu's bones lay:
sister of Gawain, mother of Mungo, lost now
beneath shops at the mall that bears her name[22]
where we perform the modern mysteries of wealth
and celebrate the tyranny of meaningless choice,
the triumph of appetite over understanding,

---

[22] St. Enoch Centre, Glasgow

and then we return to dwellings of mind and mud,

and eat luminous food without flavour

and raise a glass to heroes who have betrayed us,

as all eventually do, and generate the waste

by which our wealth is measured, and as the debris

and jetsam of consumption accumulates in piles,

a dog climbs up on each separate heap and barks,

and we get to choose which one barks best.

Three lives

This is the future.

These are our parallel lives,

our alternative biographies,

disaggregated but simultaneous,

sitting side by side:

curating Tamagotchi-style,

consequence-free

social media marriages

between fantasy avatars,

letting anonymity disinhibit

all the angels and monsters,

within us, watching them

mutate into each other,

and into something else

entirely new;

losing the culture flame-wars

against the radical apathists

on multiple platforms,

insisting on existing to nihilists

and teenage epistemological relativists

who condescend to professors

because they have literally

nothing to prove;

being drip-fed opiates

to curb the pain

while bleeding to death

into a colostomy

lying on a trolley

in a corridor

in a war zone

in the real world

somewhere.

The hinge[23]

There are secret chambers to the heart
not found in any textbook on anatomy.
The regular beat on the monitor is our slow footfall
as we pass by its many mansions.

In some we store treasures we visit on occasion:
unique, glorious, private repertoires of intimacy
that we unveil only in the immediate, undeniable
presence of love. In others we hide monsters:
prejudice, frustration, grudge, insecurity, self-loathing.
The door to that chamber is rarely touched.
It rests ajar, the hinge rusted stiff with neglect.

But, from time to time, it fascinates us, beguiling us
with possibility. We pick scabs of rust from its hinge,
oil it until the oil, blood red with rust, spills on the floor
and stains our hands, and we discover monsters
need no invitation once the door will open easily,
and are dumbstruck and paralysed with horror
as they swing grinning on the hinge.

---

[23] First sketched the day after the murder of Jo Cox.

Cuneiform[24]

Everything lies in ruins. This Glasgow

is an ancient ruined city by the Euphrates

after some rival, or barbarian invasion,

or simply the passage of time, has had its way,

gap sites where ziggurats once stood, shards

scattered across the brownfield yesteryear

whose damp tubercular breath

condenses on the back of my neck.

but this is the Clyde, not the Euphrates.

This shattered and scattered clay

whose pieces you pick up and hold

is not some Mesopotamian jigsaw

of the sort archaeologists like to solve.

These marks are not cuneiform pressed

upon the cold hard fragments in your hand

that you try to fit together and decipher.

It is you. It is your own living tongue

after it has been turned to stone,

---

[24] Written after the death of Tom Leonard

and after the sledgehammer and wrecking ball

have had their way, and broken you,

and dumped all your words in a midden

and left you able to meet your mute self

only behind glass, in a glass case, in a museum,

reading how others have captioned you in labels:

their interpretations, educated guesswork,

accidental errors, deliberate falsehoods, lies,

in some nostalgia palace

where the passage of time is frozen

to hold the living captive,

saying, "this is how things were

so this is how they will always be.

This is all in the past. It cannot save you.

You are only what we say you are now."

The word "no" lies untranslated

on a cuneiform tablet out of reach, hidden

behind something lurid and embarrassing.

but there was a man who turned it back

and raised your words from bones and ash,

lifted them from this disintegrating clay,

breathing life into them with poetry,

restoring their voice and making them laugh,

and bulldozing museums with basic facts.

Though all that's left of any life, once gone,

is an unfinished jigsaw, its missing pieces

now forever lost, we'll fill the gaps

with pieces of our own rescued from obscurity

and the impertinence of casual oppression.

The two masters

There once were two masters:

one whose teachings were universally understood,

and one who made no sense to anyone.

The first was praised as a genius.

His imperishable words illuminated the age.

People fell to their knees when he spoke

as though he had read their minds.

The other was ignored by all but one

who devotedly wrote down his teachings

even though he didn't understand them.

The age ended in turmoil.

The palace burned. The people starved.

Invaders ruled for generations

until the old language was forgotten.

One day a fragment was found.

Scholars studied it meticulously.

convened meetings to compare findings.

established entire disciplines to interpret it.

but try as they might.

they could not determine

to which master the teaching belonged.

Low winter sun

I visit the New Guardhouse[25] at night.

The monument moves me unexpectedly.

The black haphazard tessellation of its floor

seems to shift in my peripheral vision

like a lake of ink, or tar, rippled by a breeze,

so that I hesitate before I set foot on it,

to discover, as I walk upon soil gathered

from battlefields and death camps,

and over the anonymous bones it contains,

it is the calm surface of a deep well of grief

and I enter the silence of the place at last.

Morning. I turn left out Unter den Linden,

pass the Holocaust Memorial[26] on my way to work,

late among the last dregs of rush hour,

but today the low winter sun rests on the stelae,

turns them into bright slabs of light,

and I must pause

---

[25] The Neue Wache, home to the Central Memorial of the Federal Republic of Germany to the Victims of War and Tyranny

[26] Denkmal für die ermordeten Juden Europas / Memorial to the Murdered Jews of Europe

to consider the different kind of monument

the sun has made of them. We know enough

to know we are not all that we should be.

Never let that make us less than what we are.

The coup

Strange times,

when I find common cause

with you now,

who found common cause

with my opponents hitherto,

but these are the times we live in,

and the things we now must do.

Let's finish this obscenity together quickly

so that we might politely agree to disagree

about trifles once again.

Advent[27]

No room at the inn. No shepherds. Neither wise men nor angels.

No new star to follow. No glory to announce.

No peace on Earth or goodwill,

but definitely a Christmas message,

or, rather, a question, for all of us:

why do we allow a child to be touched by poverty,

loved by her refugee mother but neglected by society?

"Lord of the Landfill, Junkyard Jesus," she implores,

"let our cardboard manger, our disposable baby box

scavenged from discarded trash for my baby,

whom this world treats as if he is just as disposable,

not fall apart in slack drenched tatters

to collapse limp in this muddy trench

beneath the cold, hard November rain,"

while prematurely festive crowds gather,

distracted by discounts in distant shopping malls,

---

[27] On seeing a picture of a Syrian refugee mother using a cardboard box as a bed for her baby in Idomeni Refugee Camp, Greece, outdoors in November 2018

to consume the box's erstwhile contents

at bargain basement prices beneath the neon star

of another Black Friday, celebrating

the unremarkable miracle of the cost.

Or do you announce Yourself, God,

only to those who watch laptops by night?

Are You a viral message now? I always wondered

Why someone who's immortal would amuse Himself

with people whose entire morality

is predicated on awareness of death.

Is that why we had to kill You, God,

disguising our indifference to others

in our rejection of You?

Unless to You we're still nothing more than animals

– a reasonable conclusion given the daily proof we offer –

no better than those slack jawed beasts chewing winter fodder,

oblivious to what was happening right in front of them

in a stable one night long ago.

Gymnopédie[28]

"Bear the wounds afflicting you with grace
and spend your anger in constructive ways.
We do not know the stories that could be told
by those who hurt us, and for our part,
they won't hear ours unless we speak
considered words calmly with compassion.

"Be the measure of yourself my son.
Do not be content to satisfy others,
but make your own mark at the range
and fire until you hit it, and in life,
always find your aim within yourself
and persevere even when mocked by others
who abandon theirs for comforts more brief
than the indelible knowledge of becoming
all you want and can and should become.

---

[28] Written in March 2016 in response to unaccompanied child refugees who arrived in the UK seeking asylum and were the subject of the "Dubs amendment". Dedicated to all the orphans and unaccompanied children of war, and to their fathers.

"And this at last: always know you are loved.

When every tongue that would announce it

has fallen silent, and is corrupted and forgotten,

still, love remains, and no matter where you are

I will be there."

                    With that

the boy's father finally succumbed

to shrapnel and blunt reperfusive shock

among the ruins of the home they once knew,

leaving him in the arms of the night

to face the desert and the darkness

and the journey

alone.

The little birds

Ten thousand little birds one day
decided they must fly away.
No mummy bird or daddy bird
was there to give a guiding word,
but seasons turn. They could not stay.

The journey, it grew hard and long.
As hearts grew heavy, wings grew strong.
Some men said what they did was wrong,
and so they sang a lonely song.

One third were shot down in mid-flight,
another captured in the night
and caged and sold for the delight
of men who don't know wrong from right,

so barely one third reached our shore.
I wish that there was many more.
We welcome them with open arms
and promise to preserve from harm
these little birds escaping war.

Brave[29]

Fighting may be brave,

but dying is braver.

Not dying gun in hand,

charging into a fight you picked

to find a death you crave

"facing fearful odds

for the ashes of your fathers

and the temples of their gods[30]."

a death that garlands your grave

with glory, but dying in your bed

bombed while you sleep, instead,

without the consolation of purpose,

or while awake, sleep walking

towards a common fate whose name

redacts your own in all the books of men,

---

[29] Written on Holocaust Memorial Day 2017 and dedicated to the thousands of elderly survivors of genocide living today in Israel. There are higher rates of poverty among holocaust survivors than among the general population of similar age.

[30] From *Lays of Ancient Rome* by Thomas Babington Macaulay.

and braver still than these is life

when all you love is dead,

and just to breathe is to drown

in the decades of fresh air their grave became,

so complete was the disposal of all trace,

and when everyone thinks you are a coward

(and what's worse, doesn't say it to your face)

and you yourself think you are a coward

just for surviving, then to live

is the bravest thing of all.

Zapruder 313[31]

They tried to resurrect him

by running the movie of his death in reverse.

Tears flowed up,

and were sucked in by ducts

in the corners of the mourners' eyes.

The widow's matrimonial bliss was restored.

The gun swallowed the bullets

in a great greedy gun-muzzle guzzle,

while the driver of the open-top limousine

had to steer backwards through the plaza

using his rear-view mirror.

The laundry did itself, which was just as well,

because blood stains are very difficult to get out.

The assassin suddenly remembered

other ways to pursue his grievances,

and rediscovered optimism and faith in humanity.

---

[31] The Zapruder film is a silent picture sequence shot by Abraham Zapruder with a home-movie camera as US President John F. Kennedy's motorcade passed through Dealey Plaza in Dallas, Texas, on November 22, 1963. Frame 313 of the film captures the fatal shot to the President's head. Zapruder insisted that frame 313 be excluded from publication.

and decided to take in a movie instead.

The limp stems of once wilted bouquets
stiffened, and dead flowers burst back into bloom,
and regressed to bud-hood, and returned to seed,

but somehow, they couldn't ease the ache and grief,
refill the dust dry goblet of his generous heart,
or piece together the jigsaw of the skull
that once contained all his clever thoughts.
They couldn't find the bits they needed
to put him back together again.
Something was missing.

They reel back and forth, rewind, playback,
in an eternal tortuous slow-motion search
inside the camera that captured the moment
now lost forever.

Somewhere else

that single missing frame is all there is,

and endless spools of alternative realities

are extrapolated from it, looping,

bifurcating, dangling, splicing, and spilling

all over the messy floor of an editing suite

where all the happy endings are made.

Baby 59[32]

Your second birth was very public.

You were excavated from a tight, narrow trench,

an entirely unexpected, accidental uterus, and emerged

into the blinding brightness of the spotlight.

Rather than the warm wet glow of the womb,

you were retrieved from the confines of a cold, dark drain,

and instead of a telephone call from a new father

to grandparents and aunts and a small family circle,

the announcement of your rescue

was instantly broadcast around the world

evoking the most desperate hopes and fears

of total strangers, revealed and released, like you,

from the darkest of all possible places

in our febrile, over-stimulated imagination

where this parody of birth paraded itself

in pride of place as prelude to the procession

---

[32] "Baby 59" was the initial designation given to the new-born boy found wedged in the sewage pipe beneath a shared bathroom in a residential building in Jinhua, Zhejiang province, China, in May 2013.

of our worst nightmares.

Little one, your journey through the filth and narrows

took you through places we prefer not to think about,

where we conceal inside ourselves seeds of secret sin,

and the fear of helplessness and annihilation.

Go back far enough though,

and are we not all the children of cannibals?

Every inch of this Earth aches with ancient atrocity.

We raise crops in soil rich with rust and blood.

Ploughshares and swords may split our tale

into the separate, neat pages of our story,

but the bread we break today is plunder,

the air we breathe sucked from a long dead lung,

its last breath all that's left,

the words it carried long, long forgotten,

and there is no path we can ever take

without walking in the steps of Cain.

We ourselves are proof there is no point of no return,

and no dark and narrow straits can keep from us

the discovery of love, enduring and transcendent,

waiting in the light beyond the world's worst mire,

even in this disposable epoch, this throwaway age,

that stalks the sewers with the appetite of Saturn

mad with hunger for want of children to consume.

Post-truth

"Make no mistake. There is no freedom

but the freedom to prevail. There is no truth.

There is only the need to obey.

"We are not here to persuade you with facts.

Facts are not fixed. You nudge them and they shift.

They are rallying points around which we can gather,

and banners beneath which we march, and, make no mistake,

we will trample all your precious little truths underfoot

if we have to.

"We are all liars. So are you. Admit it.

The money in our pocket is debt.

The land of our birth was stolen.

The gods we worship despise us,

and there is no hypocrisy, none,

with which we are not defiled,

no father's sin to which we are not heir.

So, make no mistake,

we will crown a liar king

and believe every word he says

if that lets us, even for a minute,

even for just one sweet, blissful minute,

believe the lies we have to tell ourselves.

Don't try to stop us.

"Our plan is not based on information.

It is based on intention. It is simply what we will do.

Nothing more. And make no mistake about our intentions.

This would not happen in peaceful times,

and we will pick whatever fight it takes,

borrow any tired old voice of outrage

and make it render itself hoarse for our cause.

Join us or we will come for you, and when we do

we will make no mistake."

Gaza

In Gaza babies see a second birth,

born from the body then born from the earth,

the innocent witnessing their stillborn guilt,

born living then pulled in a caul of dust,

from ruins of the homes their fathers built,

as innocence departs to skies above,

where bombs fall as if from the wings of doves,

the drones absolved, the blind eye turned by us,

an innocence that we are guilty of.

הָעֲקֵידָה / The Binding

Abraham bound Isaac upon an altar

and the angel of the Lord came

and stopped his hand. Today

one child of Abraham binds the other.

and there is no angel to stop it.

The living

They are the most alive who know it least:

the children playing in Aleppo's streets,

carefree, and then most cruelly made aware

of life by its sudden end beneath

a cracked and concrete sky. And from now on

what we call life is just a kind of death.

Poppy[33]

Remember all the men who fell,

                               and women too,

and pin a bloom in your lapel,

                               of scarlet hue,

but do not celebrate their war,

presume to know what they died for,

and make this emblem of its gore

                               the next one's cue.

Don't let remembrance' solemn band

                               lure and recruit

those kids too young to understand

                               to make salute.

Don't wave the flag and beat the drum,

to rally all tomorrow's sons

and daughters to wars yet to come

                               to follow suit.

---

[33] Written on seeing a photo on the British Legion website (since removed) showing smiling children wearing 'Future Soldier' t-shirts and holding giant poppies.

Sing mud and blood and shame and pride.

                                        Sing want of sense.

Sing school friends gunned down, side by the side.

                                        for some pretence.

Appal with tales of hazards dire
in fields reduced to dub and mire
and decorated with barbed wire

                                        your audience.

Evoke artillery's hellish choir

                                        all out of tune

bombarding with anthems of fire

                                        deafened dragoons,

machine guns beating out of time
where ragged ranks dance in a line
and in the wire, their arms entwined,

                                        fall in a swoon.

148

The fingerprint

Osip sang[34] of his Kremlin man, his mountaineer

with a thick poking finger pointing the way ahead

for his menagerie of sycophantic porters. He wasn't alone.

All the world's capitals boast their climbers now,

wherever a flag can be flown in hate to claim a state,

and from the pinnacles of their mighty achievements,

from mountaintops remote and inaccessible to lesser men,

they seek to join hands with each other over our heads

as if holding a seance in which we are the spirits of the dead,

the anonymous ghosts of their future victims,

summoned and interrogated by democratic rituals

which they tell us are evidence of our consent,

then, having served our purpose, we are dismissed

to occupy the graves they have prepared for us

in accordance with the will of the people.

They reach out towards each other urgently,

strenuously exert themselves, stretch,

willing their fingertips on beyond physical limits,

each standing on tiptoe on the separate summit

---

[34] Osip Mandelstam's Stalin Epigram

of their individual boasts, their own conquests,

their unique struggles, their profound insights,

their paths to glory, their rags to riches tales,

all now aching to touch so badly, and join hands

and form their criminal club of vindicated outcasts

and misunderstood tyranny, invoking secret magic

as they extend their arms so far towards each other,

that their straining hands summon strange blossoms

emerging weirdly from beneath the ground, far below,

attracted by the broad magnetic palms of those mighty hands,

stems twisting and pushing up through the soil of the plain,

blossoms trailing smoky stems, tipped with smooth metal buds,

launched thrusting up towards the sky, piercing the sky,

pushing on towards to the stars,

and bringing all the stars back to earth with them when they fall.

And then I see they are not the only ones, these mountaineers:

the mountains they have ascended are themselves made of men,

not rock, their piled limbs greased and gleaming with sweat

as they struggle, climbing over each other to reach the top,

writhing like time lapse insects, or atoms in slow motion,

indistinguishable from each other

in the Brownian motion of their politics,

taking turns to establish themselves in temporary prominence,

occasional Pierrots in a carnival of constant overthrow,

while truth remains a beggar on the courthouse steps,

and the foaming crop of flowers carpeting the plain below

is suddenly formed now from a sea of strange bulbs of light.

The plain is frothing with little bubbles, rising, swelling,

then suddenly bulging like balloons inflating with blinding light,

bright bulging bitter fruit erupting and bursting open

on branches of trees tossed and teased from tiny subatomic seeds

cultivated in a lab somewhere by tame toiling boffins,

buffoons hot-housed in some sterile academic ego factory

insulated from each and every moral compass and consequence.

They do to humans what Pavlov wouldn't do to a dog,

performing tiny test tube apocalypses to a captive audience

that oscillates between rigid electrified attention

and slouching in exhausted and indifferent amnesia

at the flick of a Milgram switch, secretly installed

in every miraculous, mesmeric handheld device they carry

to mediate, filter and attenuate their ration of cruel reality

with an illusion of benign rationality

that makes it bearable to the infantilised mob

and facilitate the silent automated applause

of a thousand strangers' thumb-jerk response

once the final performance is unveiled

and we are our brother's keeper

only in the sense Zimbardo meant in Stanford Prison,

only in the sense

that we are all just preened and painted comfort women

draped as decorative and distracting embellishments

on the arms of disposable cannon fodder men

marching until it is as if they never existed,

only in the condemned and uncommon sense

that makes no sense and makes everyone wrong,

and there is nothing worth fighting for anymore.

And then I see it is not love that moves these mountaineers,

not love that compels them to reach for each other

as the ripe bright blooms of light on stems of dust rise

from soil rich with our own powdered and anonymous bones:

the mountaineers reach towards each other across this wide world

not to join hands or embrace, but to take each other by the throat

and as they extend their hands, they reap their crop of hate,

their stroboscopic harvest, their uranium bouquet,

and woo each other with a darkening romance

recited on tongues of ash among the fallout.

But neither is their hate sincere

for they know nothing about each other.

They ascend interior peaks on which no suns rise.

in a primordial solitude of fear and guilt and transformation.

a private Shasta and Kailash and Schiehallion in the mountains

that range secretly along the ridges of the secretions

in their own fingerprint

where with lonely heroic struggle they overcome doubt.

shut traumas that stunted their development away in caves.

defeat fantasy demons instead.

and find the severe conviction necessary

to usher into this world their internal night. their verklärte nacht.

and at last the hands unjoin. the outstretched arms fall.

the fingers descend on the button

and imprint upon it the map of their derangement

with residues of endocrine secretion.

and the missiles are launched

and the fingerprint remains on the button.

for a few minutes at least.

standing as brief testimony of an individual presence

before it evaporates in the white anonymising heat

of an artificial sun.

Oath of Unallegiance

I will not be bound by any oath.

I pledge allegiance to the unaligned.

I promise to question every value,

and uphold the sovereignty of doubt,

and all her lawful heirs and successors,

no matter what the consequences.

I salute the rag with which I blow my nose,

and scorn every frontier, cross every border,

and then make every ditch I find a Rubicon

with which to irrigate your indivisible territory.

I affirm that I will hold my duties in disdain,

and leave absent any office

that you should presume to bestow on me,

as though there had been a break in,

and you will have to frame your laws most subtly

to pretend my actions in any way imply obedience

for I will be a moving target, slipping from their aim,

eluding the cross hairs of every constitution

escaping the net of all its amendments,

for you will not govern me,

so help you, Almighty God.

Grenfell

This police line between them and us draws a line under things.

And as we shuffle and mill about at the perimeter of disaster
it reminds me of Hillsborough,
only in so far as it is yet another instance of that fault line
which runs through our society, one more bloody example
where one was more than enough:

the fence line against which the faces
of doomed football fans on a Saturday afternoon
press themselves onto the front pages
of our Sunday morning papers;

the front line along which trenches
and barbed wire decorated with corpses
of school friends machine gunned side by side,
twist and wind over the mud of Flanders,
and across the map of France;

the fault line that shifts almost imperceptibly
to cause a minor earth tremor

that brings a man-made mountain

down on the heads of the children of Aberfan

while leaving the playing fields of Eton unspoilt;

the bottom line pulled across our throats like a razor

by wealthy plutocrats, reaching down from their penthouses

high above the law,

levitating 24 storeys above the 24th floor of the inferno

holding us hostage in homes ablaze with poverty,

insisting we share this fate they have decreed,

this austerity they have condemned us to;

the telephone line over which the voices of the dead are heard,

faltering as they take their last smoky breath,

trying to say goodbye and falling silent, one night in June;

It draws a line under things. Grenfell must stand

as a charred black tombstone for all the victims

of lies and broken promises, and its fires

must light a beacon in our mind:

a beacon for all the ghosts of dead refugees

sunk to the bottom of the Mediterranean Sea,

their fumbling shades still seeking our shores,

groping through the cold dark abyss

as that false dawn filling the London sky

in the early hours of a June morning,

guides them towards those who went before,

now come back to meet them in the grave

and tell them how we burn down their homes

before they can take their place in them,

how we murder hope and all journeys are in vain;

a beacon for all who our society punishes

with poverty and hunger and wars

and catastrophes not of their making;

a beacon that guides all of us towards a common destination,

one night in June, to shuffle and mill about

at the perimeter of disaster,

a place prepared for us by neglect and ignorance

and prejudice and greed and cruelty, waiting just on the other side

of the line between them and us that draws a line under things,

and in the end none of us will survive this.

The magic money tree

It sways there in the humid breeze:

                                                 a leafy palm,

whose shade extends across the beach's

                                             pristine sand.

Great coconuts stuffed full with cash –
the civil list, the arms contracts,
the tax dodge and the offshore stash –

                                           slowly expand.

They dangle where, high on the bough,

                                        the poor can't reach,

yet drop into the open laps

                                        of high rank peers.

Here corporate donors and their friends
can hide away their dividends
until they work out how to spend

                                        what's profiteered.

Their Caribbean country club

                                        is exclusive.

Resort. tax haven, trading hub,

                                        it's conducive

to private pacts behind closed doors.
dark money deals, election fraud.
The public good is bought and sold

                                        to make them rich.

Outside the migrant and the poor

                                        throng at the gates.

Hillsborough. Grenfell and Rochdale.

                                        demand their say.

The rich instruct security:
"we do not care about their needs,
and there's no magic money tree.

                                        Turn them away."

Condemned

All of us are condemned, for should I meet

an arms dealer walking in the street,

I'll kill him with a random cobble stone,

with which I'll crack his skull and break his bones,

and whisper to his corpse through gritted teeth

"I got the stone I killed you with for free!"

suspending morals for a moral end

and like the man I kill I'll stand condemned.

The event[35]

We never learned anything

because it was not a lesson.

"It was not a learning experience[36]."

despite all the fine speeches

delivered by latter day leaders,

talking about "lessons learned."

and promising "never again".

We remain just as we were,

no better or worse than before,

except in one single respect: loss.

As people we are ghosts,

melting celluloid, mildewed archives

becoming unrecognisable shapes,

electric outlines flooded with static,

white noise providing disruptive colouration

to camouflage us for centuries to come,

remembrance attenuated by millennia,

---

[35] Written following Holocaust Memorial Day 2020
[36] From "Words of ambivalence for Holocaust Memorial Day," David Hirsch,
Goldsmiths, University of London, January 27, 2020

our names now just words hissed in lost languages,

our very existence kept alive in our obscurity

only by a covenant with the unnameable.

They said if only we remember,

then memory itself will become a kind of hope,

the simple, desperate hope,

that the likelihood of repetition

will somehow decrease by a decrement

that is incalculable, but can be wished for,

but what hope is there for what has already been lost.

No. We remember for the sake of remembering,

and for that reason alone,

for if we have learned anything at all,

if these events, and all the endless variations

on the theme that they establish, littering the histories

we sweep away with the turn of a page

at the end of the day, with our own anonymous ash,

in some uncertain future,

if they have taught us anything at all,

it is that memory can serve no other purpose.

World service

It whispers, sibilant, static
hissing snake insinuation
after the broadcast ends.

a monsoon of sound, deposited
afar, in a garden, time zone aglow
with shortwave bandwidth aura.

forming the late-night halo
of a post pub pass out
among the sofa debris

and erotic disappointment.
Exotic familiar takeaway
in hand, half eaten, comfort

after the no show, she turned it on
for company. Now she sleeps
as the bulletin begins again.

In a remote province

of a distant dictatorship:

official denial of an outbreak.

Quarantine

I look forward to the obesity,

and the alcoholism and divorce.

I look forward to the inevitable

rash of excruciatingly bad novels,

and I will read them all,

each and every self-published word.

I look forward to a plague

of unplanned pregnancies

instead of this. Instead of this.

Instead of whatever this is,

I look forward to life

telling us we are alive again.

At first, we worried that nothing

would ever be the same again,

and then we worried it would,

once we understood

the way it was had been

the problem all along,

and then we stopped caring,

living life day to day,

Irritation and inconvenience,

fear and uncertainty,

congealing in the gut,

like an indigestible cyst,

a benign tumour, a tremor,

a pulmonary premonition,

a cardiac ecstasy of awfulness,

a kind of spiritual ballast,

internalising our quarantine,

turning it into something

that would stay with us forever,

even once the shadow of the angel has passed,

lingering, not like a memory or instinct,

because there is nothing less heroic

than surviving pestilence,

but more like something blocking the sink

to stop spiders crawling up the drain:

that is how the hours pass, and the days,

and victims think of the tow paths

and the lonely places of their escape

while trapped in quarantine with the fist,

and look forward to the obesity,

and the alcoholism and divorce,

and look forward to the inevitable

rash of excruciatingly bad novels,

and will read them all,

each and every self-published word.

Bug

I'm hyper-vigilant

and socially distant

and see people as a threat.

so I meet this bug

with a shoulder shrug

because we've already met.

This quarantine

is where I've been

all the days of my life.

You're so surprised

because your life disguised

the way that these bugs bite.

Alphabet

A is for Asteroid, up in the sky,

and D is for Dinosaurs, all of whom die.

B is for Brexit realpolitik,

and C is for CoViD that makes us all sick.

E is for Eejit and F is for Fuck,

and G is for Get To. We drop H a lot.

I is for I'm All Right, J is for Jack,

and L is for ICU beds that we Lack.

K is for Kindness amidst too much Greed,

and M is for Miracle. N is for Need.

O Obviates unforeseen force majeure,

while P is austerity, making us Poor.

Q is for Quarantine. R is for Risk,

and S is for Stockpiling selfish wee pricks.

T is the death Toll that grows and climbs higher,

and U exponential growth of Unforced error.

V is the shareholder Value that's saved

as millions of insurance payouts are Waived,

and X the eXcuses the government gave.

Y is a question going round in my head,

and Z is a letter that rhymes with dead.

We live in the ruins of what might have been

We live in the ruins of what might have been.

We are correspondents reporting wars waged on ourselves

now we have forgotten how to disagree with each other.

Competing truths are banners around which to rally

in the twilight of our civilisation,

their contradictory demands shattering the prism

that would refract them, our discourse so degraded

it no longer accommodates difference without rancour.

Questions make you a proxy target in the crossfire:

we live in an age where doubt has become painful

and everyone seeks the reassurance of false certainties

and clamours for lies while damning the Lügenpresse

that threatens their Tausendjähriges Brexit

and we live in the ruins of what might have been.

The sea

The sea does not end on Lesbos' shore[37].

I found it yesterday in Hamburg Hauptbahnhof[38]

in the eyes of the woman to whom I gave my sandwiches

before I remembered what was important

and ran to make it to my meeting on time.

but last night, safe at home,

thinking about my day, I found the sea again,

in my eyes this time.

---

[37] Where refugees in Mória Reception and Identification Centre have reached land after crossing the Aegean sea.
[38] Written after meeting Syrian refugees begging in Hamburg

Earthquake

We thought we washed our hands

with water, not knowing transparent blood

ran crystal clear from the open wounds

of all the worlds we had killed.

Innocence was our guilt,

our crime so complete

that even knowing of its commission

was blasphemy. Imperceptible shifts

in our tectonic virtue - seemingly solid,

yet resting on molten rock - accumulated,

gradually, until the inevitable cataclysm,

which was attributed to an arbitrary,

and inscrutable deity, whose anger

was, at the same time, our absolution,

reliving us of all responsibility,

given we had no-one to blame

but ourselves.

Kino II

We glamorise the void so that we can recruit monsters from it

with a clear conscience, raising celluloid and silver screen

to mark the perimeter they patrol, the vanishingly thin membrane

that divides the darkness of the auditorium

from the bottomless pit on whose brink they stand.

While we sit distracted and safe and soda-bloated

they stand, drenched in blood like greasepaint,

converting carnage to farce, breathing fire

into balloon animals that turn on us and maul us,

but while they perform the alchemy

that turns fear to entertainment,

before retreating back into the abyss

from which we summoned them

as the credits roll and the theatre empties,

returning on cue for the next screening

as the programme dictates, imagine how they regard us.

Imagine the void we represent to them,

the horrors we portray in our indolence,

our eloi-indifferent indolence, and be grateful

they don't stride off the screen to slaughter us like morloks.

Surfing

We're blood surfing.

We're surfing on blood,

riding waves of genocide,

from Plyazh beach, Mariupol,

to Al Deira beach, Gaza,

until we wipe out and wash up

on some beach near Bodrum, Turkey,

oblivious to the history

that unleashed the flood

until it breaks over us,

and we feel the current tug,

and the twist and struggle starts.

We recline in the jasmine

of an atrocity garden

where bees drink red nectar.

Our ancestors' avarice

is in full bloom and smells so sweet,

that we don't think of the mass graves

beneath our feet,

and beneath them, that's not magma

on which tectonic plates slip and slide and tilt.

Trading blocs collide and subduct

on oceans of blood. We're blood surfing.

We're surfing on blood, and dreaming

of beaches you only reach by drowning.

Our corpse is washed up

and revived by cocktails.

Ambulances with minibars arrive,

offering mojitos instead of defibrillators.

We sit up on the sand, smile, laugh, stand,

and join the dead dictators at the chiringuito,

and watch the tide come in, and raise a toast

as it takes the other bodies out with it,

the bodies of poor refugees

for whom a dollar bill is not a life raft.

The long walk[39]

A dancer has taken off his mask

in front of uninitiated children[40].

I remember as a child we would go

with father to the sacred mountain,

and in its foothills visit the ruins

of the dwellings of our ancestors,

and he would visit their shrines

to speak with the intermediaries

who live among the forbidden summits[41]

whence they descend to move among us,

and brother bear and brother eagle,

coyote the trickster, mountain lion,

and sister snake watched from afar,

having their own separate audience with the gods,

but a dancer has taken off his mask

in front of uninitiated children.

---

[39] Hundreds of "Indian Removal" deportations and other death marches were a key measure in the ethnic cleansing and genocide of Native Americans.

[40] "ceremonialism will [end] when a kachina removes his mask during a dance in the plaza before uninitiated children" (Frank Waters, Book of the Hopi).

[41] Hopi kachinas are said to live on the San Francisco Peaks, Arizona.

White brothers come from the east

for a new and bitter pilgrimage,

not to the beginning of time,

among the relics of our predecessors,

but beyond the limits of endurance

to the end of the fourth world[42].

The songs that held us up fall silent.

The ancestors are struck dumb. Father

has died and fallen by the wayside

and there is no time to stop and mourn,

and bear and eagle, lion, snake and coyote

turn away from their brothers and sisters

who have fallen through heat or thirst,

hunger or exhaustion, and perished.

They turn away from the sadness,

the dances unperformed, songs unsung,

and our people will lie there now

until the earth claims their dust

and lingering sadness is taken away by the wind.

---

[42] Humanity is currently residing in the Fourth World, Túwaqachi. According to prophecy, Túwaqachi, like the previous worlds, will be destroyed because of the corruption of humanity. (ibid.)

The white brothers speak of destiny
made manifest, but they would not understand
what the dancer who removed his mask
would tell them to their face:
words that will destroy them.

There is no destiny, only a dance;
there is no plan, only a pulse,
and all things are connected;
there is no fate, no past or future,
no failure to fear, no prize to win,
only right here, now and forever;
nothing is forbidden to those
who revere all things,
sin impossible to commit
for those with perfect knowledge:
they may kill us, march us to death,
erase all memory of our existence,
but we will rise again in all things,
our hymns of praise concealed
even within their most guttural insults,
our children swarming in their marrow,
and our memory will be restored at last

in the great forgetting

to which they have condemned themselves

by amputating themselves from the world.

making their journey

one from cradle to grave only.

thinking they compel us to do the same,

when the paths we walk will always be

just one of many possible trails

beneath the stars.

Our enemies may prevail,

but even in their hour of victory

they will destroy themselves,

and the spoils will be inherited

by those who met

the inevitability of their annihilation

on friendlier terms.

Vulgar fraction

I am a fraction of a person,

a simple, common, or vulgar fraction.

I am not a whole person anymore.

I am remembered only as one of many.

I have no individual existence.

The unit of which I am part, the "1,"

stands as a monument on the ground,

the virgule, the solidus, the fraction bar

covering the denominator that tells us

how many people are buried here[43].

I am one of them. I am part of this.

I am a fraction of a person,

a vulgar fraction.

---

[43] Written following the discovery of mass graves after the withdrawal of Russian forces from Bucha, Ukraine

Confiteor

Some words will turn our ink to tar

that slows our pen as we transcribe them.

Some subjects turn our mouths to scars

that gape to bleed words to describe them,

so silent we our counsel keep

that wounds are less inclined to weep.

Ask, if you hear us confess pain,

from what witness do we refrain.

The opposite of violence

You have your pain. I have mine.

All I really know about yours

is that it hurts. I can't share it.

You can never know my pain

beyond what it has in common

with yours. Our wounds

belong to each of us alone,

and yet we know enough, I think,

If we can trust, and listen, and love,

we know enough to hold each other,

to understand what we can,

acknowledge what we can't,

and undelete what crueler hands erased,

restore colour to those memories

made monochrome with pain.

and maybe I can finally forgive

those who hurt me

as I beg my own ghosts.

the ghosts of who I was

and who I hurt.

for forgiveness.

L - #0229 - 290422 - C0 - 210/148/10 - PB - DID3305768